Camino Voices
Camino Voices
Camino Voices
Camino Voices
Camino Voices
Camino Voices
Camino Voices
Camino Voices
Camino Voices
Camino Voices

Rachael,

Bon Camino

Iain Dryden.

BAY OF BISCAY
Fisterra
Santiago
Atlantic
PICOS DE EUROPA
Ponferrada
Leon
FRANCE
St Jean
Burgos
Logrono
SPAIN

'The walk is the destination, not Santiago.''

*Camino Voices is dedicated to my wife Millie,
and to all who walk El Camino.*

Without my wife's **help** in editing several times, proof reading
and a hundred other things, this book might still be a scattering
of ideas trying to coagulate in our attic.

Thanks

Many people nagged me to create this book, especially:- Viktorija in
London/California/Bali for prompting me so many times: Christine at the
cafe La Frontera in Fisterra for your unbounded enthusiasm, Antonio of the
Costa Vella Hotel in Santiago for your warm support. Thank you to the
550+ walkers I **met,** listened to and recorded along The Way. Everyone
who engaged in our market research really helped. I would like to extend
my special thanks to Verna and Jo & Mario for their precise editing and
spot-●n advice. Thanks also to Penny & Julian, Dauda and
Patrick for believing in this project. Thanks to **YPS** for
walking me through the mysterious publishing process.

A percentage of every **copy** sold will be donated to a Camino *charity*.

This book is printed on paper from **sustainable** forests.

Publication details are on the last page.

Some Warnings !

Evolving from a disorganised sketchbook which walkers implored I turn into a book, 'Camino Voices' **attempts** to capture the long distance walk's spirit. There are no **yellow** arrows, nor page numbers, Roncesvalles gets only a distant sketch, but there is a map of sorts. It avoids every city except Santiago, because at the edge of one, I fought off car-jackers and not just once.

My observations are in this typeface (light).

Walkers' spoken words (in italics) are nameless to represent extraordinary people from around the world. Purposefully, no record of who said *what* **exists**.

All the material in 'Camino Voices' was drawn, recorded and compiled by the author.

A preamble.

We were born to walk. We strode across Africa, we stepped over the Red Sea, we paced the coasts of every continent and then we sat down in easy chairs. If sitting is the new cancer, walking is the new super-drug.

If you can manage it, walking for about thirty-five days does wonders to your body, brain cells and spirit. Should you want proof, read the voices of those who walked from St Jean Pied de Port in France and across northern Spain to the port of Fisterra.

They flew in from all over the world, they drove from various parts of Europe and they abandoned St Jean's comforts for the incredibly steep track which rises up the nearest Pyrenean mountain. I could recognise them by their sparkling walking gear and shiny rucksacks, by the gleam in their eyes, but also from the haunted look they gained after leaving the Camino help desk where previous walker-volunteers had worried them with graphs, maps and diagrams of the walk's elevation.

But there were others. Worn clothes, scuffed and stained rucksacks, boots long worn in. These amazing walkers had stomped across France, some from the classic start at Le Puy, others from a range of towns and cities across Europe. I met a couple hot off the trail from Rome and a woman who had walked from Hamburg.

The weather in April was clear-sky cold and like all spring chicks I instantly wanted to.... No, not join the great walk, but settle in this charmed, welcoming town with an air of excitement, set in idyllic countryside backed by the impressive Pyrenees. Neat medieval houses painted white with burgundy red woodwork lined cobbled streets, enticing gardens in which you could see yourself reclining through the warm months, cafes, restaurants and shops to suit all tastes.

For years we had discussed El Camino, but as I found out more and as the reality got closer, my interest wilted. The crowds, the noise, the snoring dormitories, they didn't pull me and I was convinced Born-Again types would be keen to pollute my miserable agnostic soul, so I was glad I had a genuine excuse to pull out without spoiling my wife's journey.

Regardless of how they had slept, every morning those in the mood were off as soon as they could. In my wife's case, this was the scorned-upon hour of seven thirty. Having retired young from a dreadfully stressful inner-city hospital job four months previously, she needed purpose. Her preparation for El Camino had been to gradually increase the distance she walked  every week, until one day she steamed 28km up an incredibly steep mountain with a full pack, and she did it in six hours.

That frosty spring morning in St Jean, the intrepid walkers stomped off with their sacks filled with all they thought they needed. The odd early-rising tourist took photos of the flood of women and men which became a trickle by eight o'clock. Awed by what the crowd was undertaking, in the wake of my wife's elegant stride, I jiggled along with my crutches.

At the edge of town, a mere six to eight hundred metres away, I watched her and our friends move up the narrow road which climbed the first Pyrenean slope. She waved. My heart leapt. They were gone. What an incredible thing she and this keen swarm were undertaking.

For the next six weeks, our paths would only occasionally cross, for I was to lurk in the distance in case I was needed. Armed with pen and sketchbook, I retraced my steps and drew Porte d'Espagne, through which walkers had stepped for hundreds of years. Daunted by the detail, feeling chilly in the shade, I did a simple outline of the town gate and the style helped define many of my subsequent drawings.

I hobbled off to start our rusty old, and vaguely white VW van which my wife had teasingly nicknamed 'Le Van Blanc'. This worn-out ex-builder's work-horse was on her maiden voyage as a camper van. She still smelt of new wood from the simple Zen conversion done by a local carpenter.

 You can tell we three, Le Van, Millie and me, were, in our individual ways, taking this Camino thing seriously.

"I'm not in a hurry. The road ahead will wait for me."

She walked past, eyes set, head forwards, stout stick tapping the pavement. I took her for a pilgrim starting with determination, but half an hour later she was back. Was she lost? I pointed out the Camino route. Ignoring me, she stomped onwards. Half an hour later she passed again, heading in a different direction. Was she practising walking with a loaded pack? Perhaps she would set off the next morning. Three days later, I was back doing business and more sketches and every half hour she passed me, determined as ever. Was she OK? I dared not intrude. Would she at last join the 664 walkers the Camino passport office said would leave the next dawn?

Porte d'Espagne
St Jean Pied de Port

"Everyone prepares, reads books, searches forums etc.

Me, I know nothing, I want to experience it uncluttered, in my own way, as it happens."

"All my life it has been, fit in, don't think, work hard. At school, college, work. Now I'm retired I can think. To me the walk will be a meditation, a time to unwind, to find out what I think, to discover day by day who I am."

"I completed my PhD, so it seems right to do this walk."

I can only manage 10 km a day, so it'll be a long haul. But I won't stop.

My life is in shreds. *I have nowhere to go, nothing to do. I hope the* **Camino** *will sort me out.*

I am alive, I almost died last year, so each step is precious, *each* day *an adventure.*

Drunk, celebrating an important birthday, *at 4am I declared I'd do the Camino. The next morning I rang cancelling three months work and here I am 2,000 km later!*

Although as polite as a man in a van could be, it felt churlish driving up the seriously steep country lane crowded with walkers groaning under heavy packs. Embarrassed to the core, parking near the refuge. I found a table on the terrace. When my beloved arrived red faced from her fight with gravity, we celebrated with freshly pressed orange juice.

Above Orisson

We'd better get a move on!
Why?
Look ahead, dozens of the blighters!
But there is loads of space at Roncesvalles.
Let's rise at 4 AM to have an advantage!
No. Let's enjoy this trip.

Overtaken by somebody over-weight, carrying an overloaded rucksack and who constantly needed to rest, humbled, I retreated down the slope, stowed my crutches and drove uphill, weaving through the walkers, feeling guilty. Guilt was to be a constant until I realised I could no longer do what these brave people did - my sketchbook and Le Van Blanc were to be my Camino.

Sat upon a rock, I sketched and talked to those who
stopped to rest. One young woman slumped beside
me and said she was utterly done-in and
couldn't continue. I offered her a lift in Le
Van Blanc parked five hundred
metres downhill. By the time I
was finished she was
skipping off along the
path.

The wind, the rain, two steps up, one back, it was like a Charlie Chaplin film.

We've lived together 20 years and decided to get married at the top of the Pyrenees. After a fantastic meal in St Jean, we walked to the ridge. On the way I found a plastic bottle ring and she found a keyring. These united us, so, unplanned, we kept walking the Camino.

beyond Roncesvalles

I left my job, fed up with being badly treated. A friend had done the Camino so I'm texting her as I go.

We were woken at an early hour by a guitar and singing. After a moment's annoyance, I blinked and woke to a joy rolling around the dormitory.

Wow, the climb from St Jean was tough! Even without a backpack it was the steepest walk I've ever done. Add on the rucksack and you treble the effort. Stick on the kilometres, all 27 of them, and you are half dead by the end.

Parking on the main road, I found a seat upon the cafe's terrace, knowing my wife would be taking a shower with other exhausted walkers who had lugged their loads up that mountain path and down through a slippery forest. Instantly, the topography had changed. Behind, brooding slopes sucked the clouds, before, gently rolling farmland. For a thousand years monks had tamed this once savage landscape and the kings of Europe had given money to construct an impressive monastery not far from where French forces had long ago been defeated.

This impressive haven, somewhat austere, welcomed us and the bustling cafe was doing its best to soothe aching bodies by serving an endless stream of beer, wine and hot chocolate. I attempted to book a table but there wasn't a slot until 8.30 and that was too late for my tired wife.

I couldn't help listening-in to four people discussing their long day. One had left St Jean at five in the morning whilst the others had been more relaxed. Within five minutes I understood there was a divide amongst those mad enough to stomp this ancient route - those who counted the hours and distance and others who shunned such calculations.

Somebody sidled up to me complaining, "This partying isn't the spirit of El Camino."

I countered, "In medieval times princes and aristocrats rode this way with huge entourages and they partied and danced. They also prayed, fed the poor and gave money to build vast hostels."

Exhausted, hanging out my washing, two women asked if I had any spare pegs. I said, no, I need them all. It shocked me I'd been so selfish. It was a primitive survival thing.

Some folk, rucksacks dead clean, suitcases delivered each day to albergues, dominate the mirrors, the sinks, the showers. We, dusty, sweating, exhausted from carrying our own packs, have to wait until they were all made up.

It is truly humbling living like this, stuck together like sardines at night. You wake in the night and realise how difficult life must be for refugees. You can walk away from this, they can't. You can go out and buy food, they can't. You are safe from changes, they aren't.

I want all of my possessions *tied* to me with string so that I can keep track of where they all are.

In deepest sleep dreaming I was meditating, a brightness made me think I'd attained **enlightenment**. My eyes opened and I realised I'd been shot by a torch!

People are out of their **comfort** zone.

Zubiri

5 AM. **Rustle**, rustle, crackle, crackle, zip, **zip**. The head torches flash everywhere. Off they go to the bathroom and, returning, it is repeated all over again with whispers as **loud** as normal speaking. And certain groups go into full chat mode as soon as they are awake. AND it's **5am.**

The long empty track without trees and you're dying for a wee. Eventually modesty is kicked out by desperation.

near Pamplona

I'm an introvert and used to feel uncomfortable within groups, but you're forced to be with others, where you sleep, where you eat, as you walk. It was tough. I kept to myself, I set off early, walked fast and tried to eat alone. But gradually I settled into being around people, it happened without my noticing. Now I enjoy it. I think introversion is a result of being damaged in childhood, and being extrovert is a natural state. We are social animals after all.

A walker sat down with his guitar and began to play. Another man who had just arrived took a small table from a cafe to use as a drum.   A few bars in, a woman started to sing and soon another began dancing, she was completely lost to the music. Walkers laid down their packs and clapped to the beat. I had little time to sketch before the three performers stopped, said farewell, grabbed their packs and walked off with their individual groups. As if in a daze, the dancer watched them disappear. Her voice was faint, "I never do this, I'm so shy. That's the Camino for you!"

Alto Perdon

It's hot up here **because** somebody turned off the windmills.

The incredible thing about The Camino is the safety - women can walk alone. Well within reason - I make sure I'm within sight of others..

The key is to respect your body and walk accordingly.

Walkers were everywhere and they kept arriving as I drove into this appealing town contained within a manageable space. Understanding how special her journey was, at Roncesvalles I had left my wife to walk ahead without interrupting her meditative days. But where to find her? We'd simply said, "At Puente."

My international phone package didn't work, so I stopped at various hostels, hotels and albergues. Nobody had heard of her and it was getting late. In a cafe, I desperately sent an email and thankfully, before my cup was empty, she pinged back from a hostel two hundred metres away.

Having left a successful woman stressed out from a tough hands-on and highly responsible post in a busy inner-city hospital, I found a gleeful teenager. It took a while to adjust to this fizzy woman who'd reverted to the person I'd fallen in love with years before. When I had, I clicked what The Camino was all about.

After three days, feet aching, blisters, sore tendons, headaches, not sleeping at night, plus the weather to deal with, we both thought of giving up. But somehow we continued, doing less, enjoying the cafes, stops and picnics. The body got better bit by bit and now we're roughly OK.

Puente's doors reminded me of the ancient Swahili doors back in my homeland, Kenya. But how, in B&W, to make each door look different? The challenge occupied me the next morning as my wife and others streamed over the elegant bridge after which the town is named.

Running my own business was crazy stress. I decided to quit for a year and travel. In Barcelona, I heard about St Jean and in the church I was touched by the mass. It was then I decided to do the Camino.

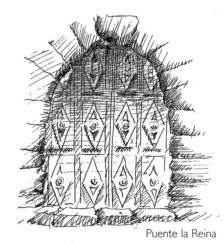

Puente la Reina

My 10 year old nephew told me: "I don't know what all the fuss is about, all you're doing is going for a walk!"

What I've found is me. That's better than a lover, better than everything.

Mid afternoon, sat outside quaint old tearooms, I was enjoying the homemade cake. Two women laid down their packs, sat next to me and ordered tea and biscuits. They were gaily chatting about the Camino when they hailed a man "Hey there!"
He slowed, adjusted his pack and asked, "Hi ! Is there a pub nearby?"
"At this early hour?"
"I need a Guinness."
"Come sit with us."
"They do Guinness?"
"It's a tearooms, stupid."
"To heck with that!" And off he stomped.

We're so slow that everything becomes cinematic, you're in a movie set.

The blisters! They kill you. They make you take a bus, then a rest day, then three.

A small group of people stood watching as I attempted to catch walkers resting or getting ready to move on. Over the far side six figures sat meditating. One of the group said, "Last night I was transfixed by that group of Buddhists. I'm a regular Catholic by the way. They were sat on their bunks meditating. I went for a shower and returning I found them as still as rock. It really touched me. They are such calm, delightful people. It is obvious they are deeply in touch with what I call my God, yet they don't believe in a God. That's got me thinking."

There's only the wind, the birds, the crunch of your boots. You listen to the level of gravel under your boots, forced to a greater involvement. This makes your day a better event.

The day off is magical. You are like a child in wonderland.

Basque villages were generally alive. There were cafes, small shops and people of all ages moved about, playing, working, chatting. I watched a muscular man tenderly lift an infant across a granite trough from which four brown horses drank. Her tiny hand reached out to a massive forehead; the horse lifted it's noble head and they looked into each other's eyes.

I put down my sketchbook after somebody asked me to take her photo. I had noticed lots of single women walking and asked if this might be a trend.

She said, "Yes. There's so much on women. We have to perform better than men at work to prove we're OK. We're expected to be great lovers, inspiring friends, perfect wives, loving mothers AND we have to look good! El Camino is a time to be ourselves without pressure. And it is safe. AND you can do it alone without a guy! Where else is that true?"

Zirauki

I saw a man with a washing up bowl tied to his backpack. That's one of the Camino's great mysteries!

When we entered the albergue there was a great discussion about blisters. After a shower, the chat had moved onto bedbugs. I made a cup of tea and took it outside to admire the view. Returning inside 40 minutes later, bedbugs was still the hot topic!!

We decided to remove the bells from our bikes and to approach the walkers at walking speed, only passing when they became aware. Our fellow cyclists embarrass us by what appears as aggression as they speed along what has always been a walkers' path.

I like my pack, but fill up with water and that 1.5 kg tips it beyond being liked.

Lifting your pack first thing in the morning, you ask why are you doing this to yourself?

Imagine returning to running a house, this rucksack seems complex enough.

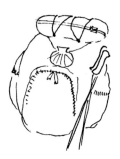

We all compare rucksacks as if we were bikers talking about our engines and tyres. There's pack envy out there. I know I have it!

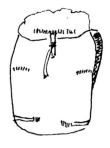

My bag never packs the same, it's roughly OK in the morning, but something goes wonky when I take out an item later in the day.

Wearing a backpack for so long has stopped me slouching and its also improved my troublesome back.

Dwarfing their packs...
good on them.

As I drew, walkers kept fiddling with their packs, but that is one of the challenges of drawing. With a camera you stand back, click and move on. Drawing holds you there for as long as it takes. An advantage is that people don't stiffen up, nor do they pose.

One woman lingered watching me and eventually she said, "As well as carrying this backpack, I sent on a case filled with fine evening wear. That soon stopped. Imagine a woman in designer clothes amongst walkers? Ridiculous!"
"Our suitcases are in storage," her husband smiled.
"It took all evening to adjust to wearing ordinary clothes, but at least I fit in."
"We'll probably get bored of wearing the same clothes, day-in, day out."
"It's more a women thing. We're trained from infancy to look 'different'. Anyway, I realise now that looking good is more about how you feel about yourself. For me, that's a huge lesson."

near Estella

I've lost the ability to talk, words seem unimportant. We drown ourselves in words. Stop talking and life is just so **much** less complicated.

Hovering between the shrubs as if not there at all, her face was ethereal, the world and its problems didn't touch her. We made eye contact and she smiled, said hello and her voice was delicate but as we spoke her words were potent. Responding to a question, she said, "Walking is a natural human activity which benefits us on so many levels. The constant movement oxygenates blood coursing through our cells, vitalises every part of the body. Passing through nature for hours calms us and the continually changing stimulation of so many different things to look at gives a positive boost to the mind."

I had slept the night with Le Van Blanc tucked into bushes at the side of a farm track. Expecting tractors to wake me before dawn, I was rather dozy when I found a cafe and ate what was to become my favourite breakfast - toast with crushed tomato and an excellent stiff coffee with a dash of milk.

Revived, I sat down to draw and to record voices drifting past. I got into conversation with a local man selling trinkets to walkers who told me he only made enough to pay the rent, but he loved his job. He invited me to lunch in his home and we discussed his people's strong culture which has retained its unique identity despite waves of invasions over thousands of years.

It amazed me the Basques have stayed put all that time! As a farmer had exclaimed a few days earlier, "When you find paradise, why move!"

My new friend said, "The walkers lift my soul, they are generally cheerful even though they are often tired. We admire them, they inspire us, they remind us of our ancestors who did this trek before Christianity to see where the sun set."

I bought a wooden medallion of the Basque symbol, Lauburu, which has many interpretations. He explained, "It's our own yin & yang representing the sun, natural forces and our internal world."

I met someone who said, **"Walking**, you sometimes sink into step with somebody and get in touch on so many levels that you flow. One evening at a cafe things started to happen with the person I'd walked with all week, but I pulled back. Yes this person *felt* like my soul mate, but my history has made me what they see in me and a big part of that is my marriage. They couldn't understand, which ended the amity, but I came out stronger for understanding **myself"**.

looking at Monjardin

I get in and don't want to talk until I've washed my clothes, had a shower and eaten a snack.

It is when we accept, not fight them, that our realities become easier to bear, said a man partly crippled for life after an accident at work.

Come on. Time to go.
Do I have to?
It's only 6 Ks.
I don't care.
She sings - I love you my honey.
Oh ho! That does it. And up he gets.

Sarsol, Navarra.

El Camino's track wound up the hill and for a while I had the scene all to myself. It was the perfect morning and silence held me in place. Drawing, when I am thinking only of the process, calms me.

She looked tired and stopped to rest and inevitably our chatter turned to what we thought about life. She said, "All religions are outdated institutions trying to keep themselves alive."
"Like Victorian businesses," I added.
"Exactly. They build temples or churches to entice people inside, they create a brand mark to unite people under their projected medieval ethos and they can't tolerate modern mankind because we think differently."
"My religion is relationship - with empathy as its moral basis."
She laughed, "Only when you truly empathise do you properly live!"

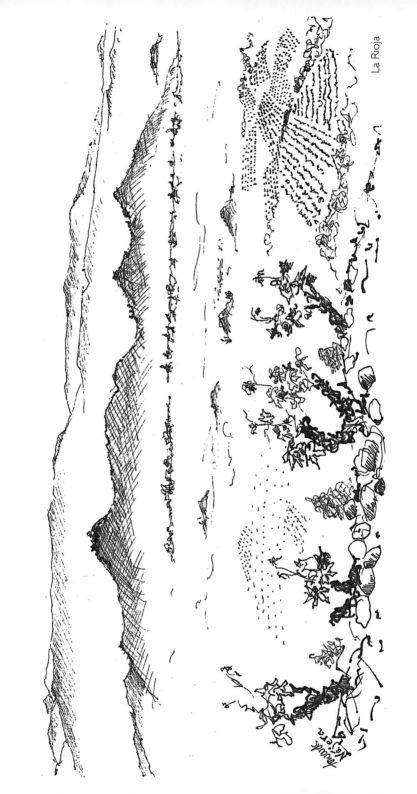

La Rioja

Rising to the crest, you enter a new world, for every valley system is different.

You may *start* the walking day all grumpy, annoyed at your stiff body or grumbling about the unfairness of this or that, but walking lifts you f r o m   s e l f indulgence and into appreciating what *is*.

I'm not good at taking *help*, but on the Camino you find you need it from time to time. It wasn't easy to admit I was as vulnerable as others.

Walking, after a while, *puts* you in *the* present ●

I came expecting nothing but a long walk. If anything, I'm pre-Christian, more inclined to admire *nature* than a god, but I've been touched and who knows *by* what.

Viana

Enjoying the urban scene and the noise of laughing children, I soon found myself talking to a couple who had a dog and a heavily loaded hand cart. The dog stopped them staying in albergues, so they camped.

"The first night a Guardia Civil told us to move from the roadside and find a campsite. A safety issue, I suppose, but I told him my wife couldn't walk a step more. Laughing, he said that was a phrase to touch the heart of any Spaniard, and he lifted a barbed wire fence and pointed to a suitable spot to set up our tent. From then onwards it's been easy."

Le Van Blanc broke down dramatically and I sought somebody who spoke English. A man who ran a hostel sorted me out and over a drink he said, "My life was in tatters when somebody suggested I walk El Camino. It cleared my head so I walked three other Caminos and finally this one again."

"What would you say to anyone doing the Camino?"

"It is all about time. People rush because they've a flight to catch. I tell them - 'In that case only walk 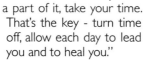 a part of it, take your time. That's the key - turn time off, allow each day to lead you and to heal you."

Time was the down side of Le Van's situation. I was forced to spend three days eating the best tapas along the trail … and testing as many delicious Roija wines as I could decently manage. And the only room in town was in the most luxurious hotel.

When the mechanic eventually rang to say Le Van Blanc was ready, I was in a pharmacy. The owner took my phone and we passed a comic few minutes as he tried to explain with hand gestures where the mechanic would meet me. During this theatrical episode, my hotel's receptionist burst in puffing desperately and gripping my luggage which she had thoughtfully carried from reception. She confirmed the info which the mechanic, bless him, had phoned her with a few minutes before. Despite her 500 metre struggle, she laughed with us and then led me to the meeting point where she waited until the mechanic drove across town to pick me up.

Along the way, I heard many such tales of uncalled for decency.

Sometimes I catch myself thinking the same old thoughts I had when working back in the city. I stop and change mindsets back to the Camino.

Navarrete

Taxis'll carry your sack to the next stage, but you want to carry it yourself. It's part of what you're doing.

I love the way the Spanish allow storks to rest where they wish, be it on a beautiful church bell tower or the roof of an ancient merchant's palace.

It's hard to imagine life exists beyond the Camino.

You sleep amongst total strangers, both male and female, a few feet apart. You quickly work out ways to undress modestly. You don't look people in the eye, you don't greet them. Close as you are physically, you each retain your personal space by holding up mental barriers. But outside everything changes - you chat, you laugh, you commiserate.

Each time I saw the storks standing like gods upon their impossible nests I had to stop. In Santa Domingo I had intended to draw something important, and the storks on the crumbling city wall looked very important. Squatting on my canvas stool I was an obstacle upon the narrow Camino trail and passing walkers would sometimes stop to survey my subject.

He sighed, "I wish I were a stork. I would fly over the Mediterranean and over-winter in Africa."

Local people also stopped and told me they loved the arrival of the storks, the birds were old friends. One person said, "It gives you faith in nature in these times when we are destroying so much without thought."

The heat was intense and walkers sat under the shade of a lime tree, drinking water from the fountain, I met my wife here after sometime apart and it struck me that she was different. The Camino, not me, was central to her existence; I was an intrusion.

What's been so impressive in this great country is that every major valley system is not only looks different, but has it's own culture, food, wine, architecture and language.

This is my 101st coffee along the way. How can you be so precise? 20 days times 5 coffee stops, plus one for the road.

She wasn't aware of this and certainly didn't mean any harm and I never took it as such.

We were on different journeys. In my van I was busy with traffic, maps and the bustle of life beyond the Camino's calm. She, on the other hand, was immersed in a prolonged meditation. All she had to do was follow the yellow arrows, find places to eat and sleep and to keep walking. Nothing else mattered; the world I moved through was beyond this narrow stream of enchanted consciousness. To her and other walkers, I was a repetitive mirage.

Viloria de Rioja

There comes a time when your body needs to repair itself. You must eat protein. You must sleep. You don't want to walk. Then you regenerate and the next day you are raring to go.

"I'm going to take the day off tomorrow because I love the rolling countryside."

A weary walker looked at her. Gathering his withering mind, he scorned, *"Day off! I walk 40 kilometres each and every day."*

She laughed. *"That's your problem and this is my lovely Camino!"*

As I worked a woman stopped to talk. She was walking the wrong way so I asked, "Where are you heading?"

"Hamburg. I was working hard and my contract had finished and that night I had a tiff with my boyfriend who doesn't think women should get tipsy, although he and his male friends get drunk each end of month. I told him I wanted to do the Camino one day and his laughter was cruel. When he said I didn't have the guts it made me determined and in the morning when he was at work, I began to pack. In the afternoon I rang him to say I was already walking and then I threw away my SIM. I've been to Santiago and now I'm walking home."

"Why again?"

"I didn't appreciate El Camino enough the first time."

Montes de Oca

Oca isn't given much prominence and slotting Le Van Blanc amongst the loaded lorries neatly aligned upon the dusty parking zone by the bridge, I could see why. Ignoring the municipal albergue upon the busy road, I was charmed by a structure built to house pilgrims in about 900AD. Having completed El Camino, the owners of what had over time become a boutique hotel, constructed a wing for the walkers. It was perfect for my wife and our friend who must have been exhausted by walking beside the busy boiling road. Sleeping nearby in Le Van B, I took supper with them in a sumptuous dining room which smart hotel guests also used.

It's the Kathmandu of the 21st century.

The Camino
is trendy.

Walking, people join
new groups. At the
regular cafe stops
they even cheer one
another in.

I've met people
from all over the
world and from
every walk of life,
it's incredible.

I love the way most
people help one
another. It's so
magical, if only society
could be like this.

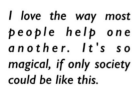

International conversations intelligently simplify English
into Globish which everyone can easily follow. How
brilliant is that!

I've done loads of solo treks in remote places for weeks on end. Here the difference is the people. That's special and transforming.

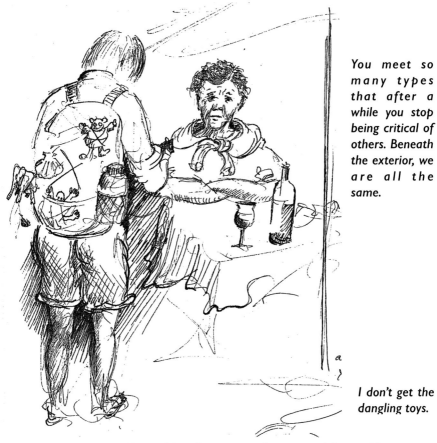

You meet so many types that after a while you stop being critical of others. Beneath the exterior, we are all the same.

I don't get the dangling toys.

The cafe was lively and I sat with a vibrant group from around the world.

"I love it, the Camino," she smiled. "Every cafe is like a party. Shattered, you drop your sack and after a stiff coffee you're in the mood to socialise."

"Me, I've fallen in love twice, no, five times," a young man winked. "Awesome. And all without a touch or a kiss because so many great people are out there walking!"

Another person added, "I was lonely until this walk, now I've made friends for life."

"Us two, we're meeting up in six months time at a music festival."

I have disconnected from

E

everything

g.

When a singing cyclist gently eases past, thanking you for making way, it makes up for all those speeding macho ones.

You've walked all day and arrive as the sun sets. Everywhere is full. What to do?

I get up, pack, walk. It's like my job.

It's like being at sea, this continued walking. You lose track of time and this frees **you.**

When my mother died, I promised I'd do Le Puy to Santiago.

above Ages

Two people waved me down; he was hobbling and she was dragging his sack. Although warned not to give lifts in Spain because car-thieves use such tricks, I couldn't help but stop.
He said, "My ankle gave out."
"But he keeps walking and it's got worse."
"We need to get to a doctor. Can you take us to Burgos?"
"Can't you see I'm going in the opposite direction."
"Look, he's in trouble."
"OK, but only to the city's edge where there's lot's of buses."
After I dropped them I got lost and at a junction, studied my map. A determined car-jacker flung open the passenger door and tried to climb in. I fought him off and drove away. Trying to work out where I was at another junction, another car-thief opened my driver's door and started to pull me out. Not wanting to hurt him, I pushed him in the chest and sped away.
So it's not always the hobbling ones ….

When you talk, the countryside slips by hardly noticed, when silent you are observant of so much.

Day after day of letting
your thoughts pass by,
the landscape settles you
into a place of peace.

M a n y   m o r e
u n d e r p a s s e s ,
footbridges, re-routing the
nasty   parts so we're
safe. That's where EU
money should go.

after Hornillos

Leaving the dust and heat of Hornillos, rising to the crest of a broad ridge, there are views across a wind swept environment upon which gigantic windmills turn lazily. Don Quixote would have been inspired, but, I wondered, would his donkey have fled in fear? A stream of walkers passed, some donkey weary, others with a quixotic bounce to their step.

Hontanas

You arrive, you ache, you massage cream in, you relax, you revive.

I can't stop eating, this is my third big meal today. Can I try some of your cake?

Many stop at cafes and get straight onto their smart phones. Others relax, and enjoy where they are.

A swallow sat chirping upon the telephone wire stretching over to the cafe which has arguably the best tortilla along the way. A woman in her late thirties sat down beside me as I drew. We chatted about The Camino, slowly slipping into an intimacy within which anything was possible. Used to this enticing magnetism The Camino generates, I didn't take it seriously. Rather, I enjoyed relating to the warm soul her bright blue eyes and electric words exposed as we sipped strong coffee.

An hour into our cosy chatter she asked why I was alone and I explained my wife was a few days ahead. She blinked. I realised we'd each assumed a different stance. Choking, she uttered that my wife must be beautiful. I said my wife might or might not be, but what warmed my life was that she was lovely inside.

Spontaneous silent tears gushed down her high cheeks. Surprised, I tried to soothe her. Embarrassed, she shook her curly blonde hair, lifted her pack and walked away. Had my words reminded her that her delicate, intelligent personality had always been obscured by her stunning beauty? Had her open heart been broken because men took advantage of both?

Nobody at the surrounding tables noticed. El Camino is a vast therapist's couch and many people along it have such moments.

I parked Le Van Blanc outside the tall wooden doors and joined my wife inside this crumbling ruin. She and our friends were blissed-out and within a short time I slipped into their mood as we sat gazing at the impressive old church. Tucked within the derelict walls was a hostel without running water or electricity and it was run by volunteers who cooked a welcome vegetarian meal which the twelve walkers enjoyed around the rough table. Touched by these gentle people's care, we shared stories or discussed philosophical points in the convivial atmosphere. Light headed from the evening, I retreated to Le Van Blanc and slept so heavily I didn't hear the dawn walkers start their long trek to the next hostel.

It is a natural part of us, doing this walk, it just happens, it's like a meditation.

I've unplugged from all expectations of myself. That's what the Camino's all about.

Castrojeriz

We chatted to two quantum physicists who happened to meet up here. This was odd, for a friend walking with my wife was a respected professor of quantum physics and so I asked ,"As scientists, what do you make of the term spirit?"
One of them answered, "It is possibly a subtle energetic charge we can feel. Everything is energy, even the atom."
"Might it not be that 'spirit' is nothing more than refined emotion?" I asked.
"Perhaps. But at a sub-atomic level, strange things happen. To me 'spirit' exists as a separate entity."
"That sounds too religious for me," the other scientist mumbled.

You have to be nuts to walk The Camino.

Got my knickers, socks 'n shirt washed 'n hung out, then a dust storm created by trucks dirtied them!

I slept on the floor. When it's that full s o m e b o d y somewhere generally helps you.

Oh the bliss of the stream on a boiling day!

Our lives are cluttered with noise nowadays. On the Camino your ears are bathed in silence, interrupted when you pass a bush bursting with birdsong. The wind carries away your thoughts, healing your soul.

The Camino crosses these eleven low medieval arches and most walkers have no idea what lies beneath their boots. I heard a cyclist approaching from quite some distance. Seeing walkers on the causeway, he took the rough vehicle track and I continued to watch him as he carefully passed those who lugged sacks up the long slope.

after Castrojeriz

Once the body

**has grown used to
the walk you can float**
*above it all and life is so, so
perfect.*

*At your wits end, after a long
day, no cafes nor shops, no
shelter - you want to lie down
under a* rock *and give up.*
**But you keep going.
You have no**

choice.

The height of this bridge hints at seasonal floods, but it was a warm afternoon and walkers looked longingly into the clear placid water, probably wishing to jump in, as did I. The lorry slowed to let the walkers move onwards at their own pace. A gaggle of cyclists stopped, took photos, loudly calling to one another because their ears hadn't adjusted to the silence after the rushing wind of moving.

Itero

Wow! The flowers and grasses, they blow me away all day long, all week long.

You can see the weather coming for hours, gradually progressing across the enormous landscape. Then, bit by bit, it is with you and you are immersed in it, but like the wind, it passes on.

She sat to watch me draw, "Back home I'm always in a hurry. I jump out of bed, shower in a rush, guzzle my breakfast, dash to work cutting corners. In the evenings I cook as if there's no time left and although I live alone I eat quickly as if it'll be gobbled by somebody else. Even in restaurants with friends.

The Camino's slowed me down. In the morning as others speed about nervously packing, I take my time. I make myself. It really helps. Now I'm a cool cookie."

I realised I'd been drawing rapidly, conscious time was passing, wishing to move on and capture the next subject. I slowed. My drawing became more in tune with where I sat, rather than where I 'was'.

near Fromista

There are those who are serious, time matters, they must get there and stop by 3 PM, they must this, they must that. Every so often I see light in somebody's eyes and stop to engage. This is what the Camino is about, lingering when something catches your heart, be it a bird, a view, a person or an emotion.

The Meseta is about accepting your fragility, your insignificance, your significance.

Most people are in their own bubbles. For them others hardly exist for much of the time.

The cyclist came rapidly from behind. I only heard him at the last second and jumped out the way. He sped past, missing me by an inch. The idiot!

El Campos

This was the Spain of legend, empty, dusty, windy, deserted villages, mud houses, great poverty which had chased the young to the cities.

The isolated trees, the grasses, the huge sky, a distance which never came closer. It was haunting. A man stopped and said he had been ordered to walk for a week by his doctor. "Doing legal work, humanity's continual folly gradually made me depressed. The pills made it worse, I had a breakdown. As I walk everything touches me and now I'm in wonderland, noticing things I never saw - even a simple stone is extraordinary."

I sighed, relishing the passing cloud of sheep.

*There are
times when
you haven't
a clue what
time of day
i t   i s ,*
even
*within an
h o u r   o r
two.*

*The sun burns. The ridge is miles off, upon it a tree.
That shade occupies your*
imagination.

He laid down his pack and slumped next to where I was sat on the ground. Once he had caught his breath, he said, "There's no cafes! I usually take a stiff coffee at the first, that gives me 3k, at the next I chase coffee with a brandy which gives me a further 5k. The max this'll work for has been 15k, my greatest distance."

I laughed, "Better than mine by 14k!"

"It's enough. I see beauty all along the path. I never want to stop, but I suppose my worn body will make me one day."

Villalcazar

The good thing is that you cover the distance quickly because it's **SO** flat.

We construct walls to defend the fragile child inside and these block us. Behind this is someone beautiful . Walking is helping me see this.

The last few villages were deserted.
Yea! Folks must hide when they hear the click of our poles.
What would we have been like had we grown up here?
We'd have fled or stayed and gone stir-crazy.
Fortunately, we'll never know which.
Ho I do, I'm already bonkers.
That's different. That's you.
Camino me!

Ledigos

They flagged me down.   Again ignoring my own experiences as well
warnings not to stop, I stopped. They instantly opened the passenger door
and jumped in, but I wasn't worried. The concern on their
faces spoke loudly. They told me they'd been meditating
and upon opening their eyes their friend had
disappeared. They'd called, they'd searched.
Fretting, they'd began walking in every
direction seeking her.

As I drove onwards, turning here and there as
instructed, she fiddled with SIM cards, transferring from
one to the other, texting, ringing, desperately worried. He
muttered their tale whilst his eyes searched, searched. We halted, peering
into every nook and cranny. Eventually I dropped them far along the way,
concerned for their lost friend. Two days later they hailed me and
introduced me to her. Bored of meditating, she'd wandered off alone.

The Meseta?
B l o o d y
boring.

A glorious section - one long meditation.

For an entire week you could see where   you were walking to. It was scary, but in the end it was rewarding.   You'd done it!

The bleakness drove me mad. I was glad of my iPad.

L o c a l s love the storks, they **even provide poles for** *t h e i r* **nests.**

You think you are moving along, it's an illusion. It's just a here experience.

A bird in the bush, it's singing filled my heart. Three loud people s t o p p e d, asked what I was looking at.

I *told* them.
They looked at me and walked away.

I felt transported by the vastness, the open skies, the rolling plains. My heart flew with the air, my thoughts touched the clouds.

I felt part of the elements, the Meseta doesn't let you escape them. The sun's glare, its heat, the cold, the wind, they are powerful and you are as nothing, so you must **accept** *them.*

The
Camino is
a river of
gold, a
stream of
purity in a
mad mad
world.

The heat is a killer.
I'm from Arizona and this ain't heat.
Well I'm from Northern Europe and it's a furnace.
Wanna burn, come 't Arizona.
No thanks.
Well, you ain't lived 'til you 'ave!
I'd rather die.

It went on forever, but there are lots
of subtle changes. I liked it, I loathed it.

The Meseta's where I'm improving my Spanish with hours l o s t   i n   m y headphones.

You've done 30 km, exhausted, in need of a good night's sleep and guess what? The town is in festival mode and it goes on all night long. The next day it takes five stiff coffees to get you on the way.

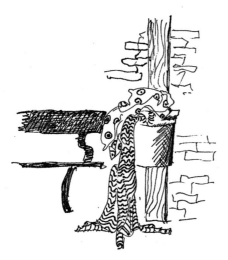

It's so simple. There is nothing to do but get to the next halt. That empties the mind.

abandoned ponchos

Sahagun

It was the morning after the fiesta. The streets were littered with paper, wine and beer were spilt across the square. Heavy metal fencing which had protected people from the bull-run encased the pavements. Exhausted workers with dark rings around their eyes swept up and washed the place. A few shattered walkers stood around trying to muster the courage to start their long day's haul after a sleepless night.

A group who had teamed up because they had the same attitude to the Camino thumbed through my sketchbooks. One of them said, "We stop all the time to enjoy what fascinates one of us - things you'd never have noticed yourself. It really opens the mind."

His friend said, "In a restaurant one day the owner gave us drinks and treated us as her own family and we stayed there all afternoon."

One or two people smell. They don't wash *their clothes daily as most do. Occasionally you* step *aside quickly from somebody who doesn't even bother to wash their* **sweaty** *bodies every day!*

You pair up with somebody and it **creates** *a link which deepens as you walk discussing the environment, sharing each other's problems, stopping to rest or retie your boots. At the cafes you sink into one another's* characters. *Then the next day it could continue or you might happen to have got up at different times so don't see each other for many days, maybe* never *again. But that's okay. It* **enriches** *you.*

I kept meeting a couple who farmed vast hectares. He said, "Here on the Camino there's birds of prey so there's loads of food for them, there's frogs in the streams and ponds which means they have clean water. That's a healthy environment. Yet there's all this intensive agriculture so they must be using less chemicals than we do."

She nodded, "That's made us **rethink**. Nature is more important than our farm."

El Burgo

Looking at the way they walk you can see who'll have tendonitis and who'll be fine.

The love the albergue showered upon you was light, humorous and comprehending of your faults. Hardened young men intent on "doing the Camino" in as short a time as possible, had softened by nightfall.

A meditation retreat lasts 2 to 7 days. This goes on and on and it changes you, if you allow it to.

Love is powerful. It erodes friction, or if the other person is incapable of responding, it enables you to let go of wanting a resolution.

Hospital

Invited to park in the hostel garden where my wife was staying, I looked on longingly as the walkers enjoyed a session of yoga. Afterwards we ate one of the best vegetarian meals I have ever had. The volunteer cook was on holiday from his real job as cook in a London vegan restaurant. Like everyone else, I fell for the place and stayed another day to help prepare the evening meal.

These people loved serving the walkers. The owner said, "They are doing a great thing and are on a long meditation, it is only right they are treated with respect."

He adopted his evening yoga so I, with damaged legs, could join in. A conservative businessman reluctantly partook and afterwards he hugged the teacher and said, "I wasn't sure about this Camino lark, but it's changing me. Yoga, loving-kindness, accepting life as it is, these were off my radar. Now I can see their point."

Great, a village! I'm gonna have a beer.
You'll only pee it off down the path.
Yep. Life's about loading and offloading.

I never admit my weaknesses, to me that's a sign of failure, but on the Camino you are bared for all to see. I found that hard, but over the weeks I've come to accept my failings. Let's hope this continues back home.

I don't sleep in Albergues. I carry a tent. I've been safe as there's only pilgrims along the way.

I forget where I start each day and who knows where I'm heading.

We rely on our smartphones to find Albergues in the increasingly competitive bed market, to catch up with others we met on the Camino, to keep in touch with friends, family, Facebook and the news.

cold early morning wind, El Ganso.

There is so little to worry about and you have yellow-arrow purpose.

The wait for the evening meal is so long - when it comes, you dive in like pigs.

A man is doing it in bare feet in the hope of curing his wife of cancer.

Foncebadon.

Sometimes I felt quite lonely as I sat sketching. Noticing me draw, two cyclists stopped and took photos of this crumbling house. I was to meet them further along the way and they took photos of themselves with me sketching.

Earlier in the day I had stopped to draw a water pump and chatted with a man playing a tiny guitar who was selling trinkets to walkers. What happens to these people when winter comes?

*You have no
responsibility,
it's great.*

**The Camino
involves a
l o t   o f
sharing.**

My chronic illness is my master.   *It has taught me to accept what I
can't change. It has opened my* *heart to those* *who suffer, which has taught me
empathy. It has* **led**   *me*   *to respect myself and others.*

*S o m e b o d y
a s k s   a
q u e s t i o n
y o u ' d
n o r m a l l y
a n s w e r
w i t h o u t
thinking, but
y o u   t h i n k
about it all
day long in
silence as you
w   a   l   k   ,
g r a d u a l l y
sorting out
t h e   d e e p
f r o m   t h e
shallow and
by the end
y o u   k n o w
w h a t   y o u
think.*

Cruz del Ferro

My child died this year and I needed to do something to strengthen my heart.

I was drawing when a woman said, "The photos make it look romantic, but so close to the road, it sucks."

Yet the pebbles carried over the centuries from around the world speak differently. Having no stone, I allowed myself to sink into the minds that had carried those weights from far away and I recalled my wife selecting hers upon a beach back home.

Acebo

She ran down the road calling my name.

I stopped sketching and wondered who the young woman was.

Unaware of my uncertainty, she told me snippets of her journey and as she did, I began to remember and then I recognised her.

The last time we'd talked she had been cool, eyes all made up, carefully arranged hair flowing over slender shoulders, classy clothes in that city fashion. Now her face was relaxed, no makeup, hair knotted, clothes simple, creased.

She was lovely - she had become herself.

Conversations
on the Camino are special,
not superficial, they're from the
heart. That makes everyone who
touches you deeply, a jewel.

We keep
stopping to
eat all those
ice creams we
did when we
were kids!

There's only you. You
may have company,
but only you can carry
your sack. It makes you
realise this is true back
in your real life, but
there you hide behind
all the things you do.

Locals along the way are
kindness incarnate. They
help with joy, they smile
with feeling.

Molinaseca

He sat down to eat his boccadillo. I happened to be drawing the bridge and couldn't believe my luck. He was tired, he said, and wanted to sleep but had to let his animal drink, however, she was frightened of the river. The donkey looked at me and I chatted with it as its ears twitched back and forth. After a while it walked around the man, peered at the water and cautiously drank. When it was done, he stood up and they wandered off to find a field.

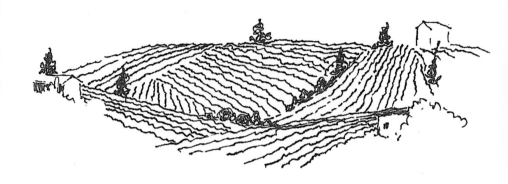

The Romans introduced vines to Bierzo's dry valley hidden deep amongst brooding wet mountains. In the albergues, cafes and restaurants, excellent and unadulterated wines made locals chuckle at Le Van Blanc's apt name.

Every day is different.

Villafranca

Many of the hostel owners are strong characters. You enter their abode and find yourself in an enchanted sphere created by their presence. They serve walkers with a delight and energy which lifts weary souls, transforming the building into a tiny spot of paradise.

I saw them enter at 8ish,
take breakfast and leave without
leaving a donation. Like many albergues,
it demands no payment, relying on the
walkers' donations. I'd seen this rudeness
before and felt irked but the owner
shrugged. "I once watched somebody empty
the donation box and walk away with all the
money others had given. But in the end it
works out - over the year we always
break   even."

*"Soaked beneath a tree, I lingered to enjoy the
rain tinkle upon the leaves above my head and
I watched wet walkers grumpily stamp past."*

It was a chilly morning and frozen from washing my torso and
face in a bucket behind Le Van Blanc, I warmed myself by
taking coffee in a bar. Two frozen cyclists leaned their
loaded bikes against the wall and stepped inside.
They sat at my table and told me they were
ashamed of some of the cyclists they saw
brutally shoving their way along the Camino.
"The walkers were here before us and
carrying those hefty rucksacks they have a
much tougher task than us."

Warmed by their company, I went off and
drew this bridge renovated in medieval times. An
old woman bearing an armful of dried branches for
her fire stopped and in broken blether we tried to
understand one another. How this made us laugh!

near Vega

above Vega

The further west you walk, the less water fountains there are for pilgrims, which is weird because the climate is wetter.

Have you seen the Camino thistles? Boggling! They keep changing. Each climate pocket has its own unique brand.

Whilst drawing this Moorish castle perched high above Vega's narrowing valley, he asked me to take a photograph and we got chatting. After a while I asked what prompted him to do the Camino.

He said, "I'd had a rough time and needed something to lift me, something to aim for. Born a Catholic, I'd become an atheist, but there's always an ethical itch inside and in Nepal I realised people who had nothing were happier than me. Like most career focused people, I'd thought I'd cracked life's conundrums."

I spend €150 a week on my shrink, but the Camino works better and it's free.

I slept outside to avoid the snoring.

This is a Camino moment. You meet somebody you'd never meet back home and enter a mental world you never thought existed. Perfect!

We'd caught a taxi to the edge of town. Unloading our packs I felt embarrassed to be seen by other pilgrims. How stupid is that?

Ruitelan

Who ever arranged the wild roadside *flowers* ought to get a *medal*. They are continually joyful, inspiring and artistic.   Good *old* nature.

Stressed trying to make enough for a big house, flash car and all the rest, one day I gave up my job and flew to Spain. After 3 days walking my boss texted me to return. I gave myself 5, then 5 more and now after 25 days I'm getting more and more peaceful. We can be content at any moment. It is here NOW, everywhere. We just don't notice it.

La Faba

I was basking outside the delightful cafe-albergue, relishing the wine and food. A man sat beside me and lit a cigarette. We were outside, it was his right, so without fuss I eased myself to the far end of the table. When he noticed, he apologised, saying he was rude. I told him not to worry, but he stubbed out his fag and I thanked him for being so considerate. He smiled and said, "All we need to do is stop and notice our effect on the world and do something positive about it. That's where happiness lies. It's that simple."

from Alto do Poyo

Does anyone mind if the window is open?
I do, it's cold outside.
But there are a lot of us in here and we need to open the window to breathe.
I'll get cold.
Can I get you a fourth blanket?
Well, I do have my sleeping bag.

Biduedo

You find yourself becoming a Camino snob. They taxi their luggage ahead, stay in hotels, taxi over the hard bits. But hey, why judge, we're each doing our own Camino!

For a couple of days I drove the rucksack of an elderly person with back pain up to the next albergue, then headed back to where I had started to keep on drawing. Each time I told her to stop walking for a few days to allow her body to heal and each time she refused. I came across her struggling along the busy but flat road from O'Cebreiro, rather than upon the peaceful but demanding path above. Encouraging her to get in, I told her to stop and rest. Her eyes filled with tears and she said, "OK, after a good night's sleep, I'll catch the bus all the way to Santiago."

a moo of cows.

Speeding cyclists barge you off
the path.
They take your refuge place for the night.
They leave late.
You, loaded heavy,
slog
and are
always last.
　　　Walkers are

bottom　　　of the

pile.

We got bed

bugs

there. They
climb to the

top bunk.

Hang your
sleeping gear
on a line and
they climb to
the top, so it's
easy to brush
them off.

Our days are like wind blown grass.

and still walking

We could cook our own food, the 4 of us. A lovely change from the usual pelegrino menu.

We have two breakfast stops and that's after eating breakfast at the albergue.

my plate of toasted peppers.

Le Van Blanc had helped somebody several times and when they called me an angel, I laughed, "No! I'm only responding to somebody in need."

They continued, "We are all angels inside, but few of us manifest it."

I countered, "I'm sure most people would have helped upon seeing you struggle."

Triacastela

Le Van B had broken down once more. And on a Sunday again. Proof she's Catholic? Again it was dramatic and it took another three days to repair, but I had a ball, sketching, making friends, eating and drinking.

There was a chilly evening breeze and I moved my chair into a spot of sun. An intelligent young person was at the neighbouring table with a hot drink and diary and we got talking. This spirited being told me, "I walk fast so tried to slow down but my body began to ache and now I'm back to being speedy. Yet I keep stopping to…" the diary opened, "look, a fallen butterfly, a flower picked off the path. Fast as I am, I 'm enchanted by so much. it is a magical journey, a long long retreat.

"I think I'll never stop walking. Each winter I return to the same permanent 3-month contract to earn enough for the year. I live simply without expensive tastes.. After reaching Finisterre, I'll walk another Camino, perhaps the Portuguese,."

I said it sounded like addiction and she smiled the addict's smile.

I have to keep busy.
It's not us, it's society's conveyor belt that conditions us.
Well, even on the Camino I push myself.
Then try to let go of it.
How?
Make yourself stop and see little things - a leaf, an ant, a view.
That sounds boring.

For over 1000 years pilgrims have done this route. But hardly any foreign walker speaks Spanish and in the hostels, cafes, shops and hotels almost nobody speaks English. That creates some amusing incidents!

dwarfing
the millions who
pass
if they notice or not.

Triacastela

Samos

This phone only texts, ideal for a walking retreat.

Rounding a narrow corner on a busy road, I had to brake dramatically. Le Van Blanc screeched to a halt. In my way was a walker loaded under a heavy rucksack. Behind this frail figure, taking up half the road, was a huge lorry braking hard. Terrified, the walker squashed herself into the thorny bushes lining the road. There was no path. This was the walker's only option. As we slid gingerly forwards the lorry driver and I smiled at the walker and each other, relieved there had been no accident.

She still haunted me as I drew this. At 30 something she had achieved more than I. Why are so many of us muddled, why do we only gain an iota of wisdom when it is too late? Why can't we be as wise as she had been aged 18?

I told another walker this and he laughed, "Our struggle to become wise is a waste of time. On this walk I have discovered that inside, beneath all my layers of muck, I AM wise. I always was. We all are. Emotional insecurity gained from parents and school has smeared us. Walking weeks on-end shakes off this unwanted jelly."

near Alto do Riocabo

What magnificence in each day!

We always leave our packs outside shops. They are safe, always. That's the magic of the Camino.

God my hips. It's as if they've been dislocated. I notice them every step but I must keep going.

One Albergue was so noisy we got up at 3am and left.

The Camino never stops from April to October. Day in, day out they start arriving at noon to ensure they have a bed. You show them around, you feed them. They sleep, you wake, clear up. They take breakfast, leave. You clean the place, wash the bedding and as you stop for a rest the first pilgrim arrives. Then there's the bookwork, the shopping, dealing with the government officials. If only I had half an hour to revive, for I want to give my best.

a cosy place to rest in Sarria

Drawing is a funny business. Sometimes you think you've caught it, but back home you realise it was a failure. Other times you think it's a mess and back home you discover you've caught it.   A bit like real life really.

The cockerels! I love being woken by them!

I was born a jewel but became a stressed out achiever and now through walking, I'm back to who we all are deep inside, but forget.

The grasses along the way have been beautiful. Before, grass was something I cut. Now it's as special as a rose.

I feel humbled by the Spanish. Such good people, such kindness, you feel welcomed.

Man! This is perfect Facebook.

near Ferreiros

*Unable to find
a bed, I spent
four nights
in the forests.
Once it
rained on
me but I
was so tired
I slept through it.*

*All day long thoughts roll around but I'm not involved, I'm on the path,
treading through nature. The days are the ideal length. I'm at ease.*

Photos in the guidebook show *fog* and rain but with this sunshine it is paradise!

The hostel owner took us to watch the sunset, silence fell on our collection of united nations.

MY CLOTHES ARE RATTTY, THEY'VE GONE GREY WITH ALL THE HAPHAZARDS OF WASHING MACHINES, BUT WHO CARES!

She is *force* of nature, the woman at the Albergue. Such passion for food for life, for people.

How far have you walked?
15 km.
Me, I'm doing **35.**
Bravo! Tomorrow I'm doing no kilometres.
What, a rest day?
Every day is a rest day, but I do end up doing some kilometres.
Ugh?

Portomarin

For the first few days I was filled with **anger** and rode rapidly along the Camino, but I got it outta me.

I hailed a cyclist.
She yelled into the wind, **"I can't stop, I'm late!"**
We walkers are never late, our feet simply tread the path.

"Our lives are enhanced by you walkers," said the restaurant owner in Portomarin. "In winter this is a dead place."
I smiled, "It looks so alive today that I can't imagine that."
"Let me tell you something. Our grandparents were ordered to leave the original town, it's down there under the water. For centuries this was a vital, vibrant settlement along El Camino - all year round we made our living fishing in the river. The dam killed generations of culture and life. People cried. They refused to leave. They had to be pulled from their homes as the water rose. So for us you walkers are a delight, something to enliven our dejected hearts."

We are each the same, yet we are different. Watching the interaction between these two has been my Camino.

A woman I had talked to before, stopped and after a while she said, "My job is a very tough one, I'm financial controller of a very large company. They gave me two months leave so I could walk the Camino."

"What has it done to you?"

"I am a changed person. The simple things are the most satisfying, life really can be easy. I want to change the way things are at work in some little way."

"The business world needs people like you."

"There are lots of big business people on this walk. And it is changing them too."

O'Cato.

We met 10 years ago on the Camino. We return regularly, for it is deep within us.

My husband died of cancer last year. I was diagnosed with it this year, so I'm on sick leave doing the Camino.

I was concentrating on the (now unfinished) tree to the left when six wealthy tourists touting huge cameras appeared. Assuming somebody drawing had the best vantage, two stood directly in front of me and three nudged behind, knocking my triangular camp stool. One of them set his camera on my head; I looked up, complained. He ordered me to stop moving.

Earlier, I had watched a group of walkers struggle up the steep bridge. Their packs looked heavy, their boots leaden. They were almost at the top when four gossiping cyclists rushed up from behind. Caught unawares by the intrusion, the walkers jumped to one side. One of them stumbled, another reached out to steady him. The cyclists shot onwards and downwards.

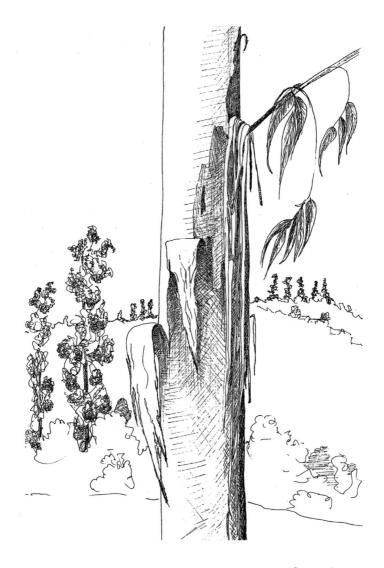

near Castaneda

Being a logical, calculating sort, I saw uncomplicated people as fools, but I've become less complex the longer I've walked and now I see they aren't naive, but often wise in a natural way.

It was har**d** retiring from the business, I'd built from nothing into being a country-wide affair. The C a m i n o h a s helped. It is s i m p l e , b u t important. You m u s t b e organised, yet you must let go when walking, so y o u e n d u p empty, but full.

*I'm the wild woman from Borneo.
Looks like I've been dragged
through a hedge backwards!*

Upon completing this sketch, I realised the subject's companion was looking over my shoulder. He hailed his friend and together they roared with laughter as they took double selfies with me as well as careful photos of the drawing. Sleeping inside the van lay a sick woman I was taking to the next town and despite the cheerful din, she heard nothing. Bounding with joy, the couple set off and each time Le Van Blanc overtook them, they'd wave and shout with abandon.

41k to go.

beyond Arzua

"I am in and out and over on top of the world and that will be it and finished."

The words of a dying child carried by his mother, (retold by another walker).

The route isn't the kilometres you've done. It's the contact with people, with nature, with yourself.

after A Calle

*We'd seen little but
tiny food stores, then
in the city we came
across a gift shop.
Like kids before a
c a n d y   s t o r e ,   w e
goggled with delight.*

Stimulated by pedestrian alleyways abounding in cafes, tapas bars, restaurants and enticing shops, my wife and I wandered past countless medieval treasures built of granite. I noticed the anticlimax of having arrived flit across her face and be replaced by wonder. We were in a dream, enthralled, boggled, euphoric. This timeless city oozed with cultural wealth, exciting people and the unexpected. I could see myself living here until the end, but I think I said that right at the beginning, in St Jean de Pied Port.

Santiago de Compostella

It is a spiritual journey, a reconnecting with all that matters.

You've become a new person on the Camino and now you need to make friends with who you once were.

So surreal dealing with Santiago. Is it real?

You really need those two days in Santiago. It is a gentle city in which to be brought back down-to-earth.

When you get to **Santiago** you go from slob to fashion creature and as you pull out that posh item of clothing, you wonder if you've not changed at **all!**

I've done it! I'm so proud of my feet, they covered every inch from St Jean de Pied Port to here. That's about one million steps - they deserve a rest!

When I go back everyone from my kids, wife and work colleagues will expect me to be who I was before. But I've changed enormously. What will happen, I have no idea.

Facing yourself all the time as you walk, day after day, you come to realise we are always alone. That once frightened me, but meeting it has made me comfortable in my own skin.

Praza da Quintana

Fento

The   Camino's

over,

you sleep long. The next day something feels wrong. It takes awhile to get used to normality.

*For me it began as just a walk. But it **evolved** into an* **inner** *journey.*

It doesn't **matter** what you believe, what matters is how you interact with things and people. Every little moment magic happens somewhere. That to you might be God, to them it's something else, but what's important is that we **allow** it to charge our minds.

I had 5 thoughts on the Camino. They fell on me and rolled around my mind until I understood them thoroughly.

Alone, looking after children and running my own business, I was stressed. **Closing** the business I've taken these past three months off as "me time". I'll go back, start a new business in tune with who I've become and see how to share the load of the children with my **ex.**

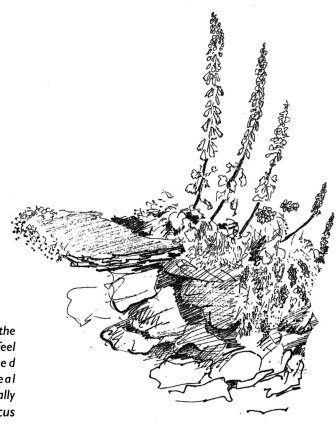

At the end of the Camino you feel d i s c o n n e c t e d from the real world. You really have **to** focus and concentrate.

The walk has abounded in
silence.

It's an endurance test and I hated most of it, but I came out *better.*

The whole Camino has been a lesson in what you don't need - physically, *emotionally* and mentally.

You meet a few people who don't seem to have got anything from the walk.. Maybe they have but are

not *aware* of it, or maybe it'll happen when they get home.

I love nature and it is in abundance *here in Spain so I'm in heaven.*

With my head plugged into music all the time, bird song was something I noticed in TV documentaries. Now it beats the beats and **toots** my day's alive.

Don't know what I've learnt, but something *profound* has happened. I can't express it, although I've tried to write it down. That means it's deep, **beyond** normal consciousness. I know it'll come out later.

Galician farmers

After three days adoring life in Santiago, my wife walked onwards towards Finisterre and a day later Le Van Blanc followed. Instantly, the land buckled and I often came across farmers walking their cattle out to pasture. Less walkers peppered the way and I was surprised how many waved cheerily, recognising me from far back down the Camino.

Negreira

The Camino is so all encompassing.

Like many of the walkers, even though in Le Van, I often felt I'd left the planet. But I came back to earth in Negreira when I spotted this monument to those who had fled poverty, hoping to make money in another part of the world.

The villages and people along the way have grown up with pilgrims flowing past for centuries. They are connected to us and we are learning we are connected to them. That's been a great pleasure.

There is a danger of being locked into a self absorbed mindset. You see people who are lost in their own world, they aren't interested in others and are quite selfish.

We met at St Jean, fell in love by Roncesvalles and have discovered each other over these past six weeks. He'll go back to his wife and family. I'll wait and see what happens.

We've arrived far too early, but we've booked the Albergue and so must stay. Is there a good picnic spot?
Yes, 1 km back along the way.
Can't do! We never go back.
OK, go forward 2 kilometres.
Good.
But you'll have to come back later.
That's allowed.

beyond Dumbria

Knowing that fires were often caused by careless campers, I parked up for the night in disused quarries or anywhere grass didn't grow. Emerging from a pit, I drew the last hills before the sea came into view, I was joined for a while by this artist who hadn't done a single sketch because he'd enjoyed walking so much. I walked onwards with him to do another sketch where the tractor is. Ten minutes later my wife popped up unexpectedly - I'd not seen her for three days and was surprised. Blissed out, she wasn't. We shared a picnic before she strode ever onwards. How I envied her being able to walk.

Cee cross

depth

pronunciation

charm

anecdotes

shifting

undergone

predictable

phone

Profound

I wish the pronunciation of letters wouldn't keep shifting with each area you enter.

The Internet, the phone, they've turned the Camino into something organisable, predictable. It used to be a chance thing.

charm

There is this man. He's all charm and chatter, but it's all anecdotes, you know - I did this, I did that. There is no depth. He is the same here at the end as he was when I met him weeks ago at the start, whereas most of us have undergone a profound shift.

I'm glad there's only one day left to go.

*Imagine ancient man getting to this
spot and seeing the sea for the first
time. To them it really was the end
of the world. What did they think?*

*I can't wait to get into a new set of clothes, six weeks
wearing and washing two shirts and trousers has had its day!*

far above Cee

Awed by what my wife had done, I waited for a group of people to stop taking selfies in every posture possible, then quickly snapped her standing at the lighthouse's 0 kilometre mark.

The Camino is over! *I feel the anti-climax, but everything comes to an end sometime.*

She was **radiant**. Having had few thoughts along the way, she'd washed away the dross which taints us humans, not that she ever had much of that.

You walk all this way and there is nothing.
What do you mean nothing! Look at that wonderful sea!
I live by the damn sea.

And Le Van Blanc was shining too - she'd made it!

We met the young woman whose wisdom had impressed me far back at Triacastela and she too was **glowing** ... and raring to start the next walk.

Me? What had happened to me. Well, the reluctant Camino-ite was hooked and being a creative spirit, I desperately wanted to produce something to represent the extraordinary phenomena called El Camino. I was longing for the beach, as was my amazing wife. So were most of the delighted

walkers whose great feat had come to an end.

looking towards Fisterra

Walking gives you a sense of freedom, it's addictive, you can see why some people become serial long distance walkers.

Those last 3 km always expand to 10 or so it seems.

You tune into the landscape in a way you can't in a car. You feel a part of it.

Along the Camino your personality is on hold. The more natural, untainted human beneath emerges. This lifts you into a zone of great peace.

Walking so far slows you down, time elongates and no longer matters. You feel you've been walking for years.

Walking you are all doing the same thing, are all at the same level and all social differences fall away.

Shadow on the sands.

Your brain goes dead, all you're doing is marching. And actually that's what the pilgrimage thing is all about, pushing yourself into this state where you transcend thought and enter a new place, like preindustrial tribal people do.

The gift of

life.

We forget how
simple,

yet how

precious

it is.

The following will soon be available on my website

Camino Posters
Buy a reasonably priced poster printed on quality paper of some of the drawings in 'Camino Voices'.

'Tracing the Flow'
A fun relaxation course based on scientific research. Couple doodling & drawing with mental techniques used by top athletes and the security forces to create a mindset which puts you firmly in control of your emotions and mental faculties.

'Satya's Truths' - A fast moving novel about a slow subject.

Unwanted adventures across northern India transform Ewan, a practical, restrained and cultured young Englishman, into a man capable of emotional intelligence. However, he must visit hell more than once, fall in love thrice and reluctantly explore the mysteries of abstract thinking. Finally, facing unpalatable family truths … he discovers who he is and realises what he wants from life.

'The Eagle's Cry' - a children's novel

Using my recorded interviews to highlight the Tibetan crisis, I created a story to encapsulate why and how Tibetan children escape to India.

Two illustrated books on iconic walks (not Caminos). To be published during 2016-17.

"Full Tilt !" Reading my brutally honest memoir, you will be glad you weren't born with my flip-flops. Smile and sweat as you follow my haphazard and perilous existence in Kenya; snigger and shiver as alone, I leave my homeland and get in to many a twist in a confusing and unpredictable world.   Out in 2016.

Beret Books   **iaindryden.com**

About the author.

Leaving Kenya aged 21, baffled by the world beyond, Iain Dryden travelled the globe, mountaineering and meditating in the Himalayas, working on boats, in factories, on building sites and selling his artwork. Giving his small art business to his employees for nothing, he worked in education, teaching geography, leading expeditions and instructing outdoor pursuits. After 12 years he went abroad to write what he nicknamed a 'coconut curriculum' for a charity helping communities encounter the 'Modern World' for the first time. Returning to England with permanently damaged health, he has stumbled along freelancing as an artist as well as an educational writer and innovator.

First Printing January 2016
Published by Beret Books
ISBN -: 978-0-9934867-0-8

'Camino Voices' and contents Copyright © May 2015 by Iain Dryden
iaindryden.com

Printed & distributed in England by YPS - York Publishing Services Ltd
yps-publishing.co.uk

Typeface Gill Sans (light & *italic*)